ESSENTIAL
MANAGERS

PROJECT MANAGEMENT

T0004396

ESSENTIAL
MANAGERS

PROJECT
MANAGEMENT

Penguin Random House

Produced for DK by Dynamo Ltd
1 Cathedral Court, Southernhay East, Exeter, EX1 1AF

Written by Peter Hobbs

Senior Art Editor Helen Spencer
Senior Editor Chauney Dunford
US Editor Karyn Gerhard
Jacket Design Development Manager Sophia MTT
Jacket Designers Akiko Kato, Juhi Sheth
Producer Nancy-Jane Maun
Production Editor Gillian Reid
Senior Managing Art Editor Lee Griffiths
Managing Editor Gareth Jones
Associate Publishing Director Liz Wheeler
Art Director Karen Self
Design Director Philip Ormerod
Publishing Director Jonathan Metcalf

This American Edition, 2021. First American Edition, 2008
Published in the United States by DK Publishing
1745 Broadway, 20th Floor, New York NY 10019

A catalog record for this book is available from the Library of Congress.
ISBN 978-0-7440-3504-9

DK books are available at special discounts when purchased in bulk for sales
promotions, premiums, fund-raising, or educational use. For details, contact:
DK Publishing Special Markets, 1745 Broadway, 20th Floor, New York, NY 10019
or SpecialSales@dk.com

Printed in China

For the curious
www.dk.com

Contents

Introduction

Project management is the skill of moving from ideas to results and, as such, is applicable to every significant initiative we are assigned or think up ourselves. Today, individuals, organizations, and nations need project management skills more than ever in a world that values individual and collective initiative above just about any other attribute.

Project Management outlines a range of practical understandings and skills that will make your projects both successful and satisfying. It will provide you with common-sense solutions to the project management issues you will face as you plan and implement projects, and the tools, tips, and techniques it contains are intended to help you achieve consistent success with minimum resources. This includes advice on the best approaches, choosing the right software, and managing projects with remote team members. Although the book is written for those taking their first steps in project management, it also offers helpful reminders to those with more experience.

In the final analysis, your success as a project manager comes down to you. It will depend on your ability to make your vision of "what can be" more influential in your thoughts and actions, and those of others, than the reality of "what currently is." If the following pages guide, challenge, and energize you in this quest, they will have fulfilled their purpose.

Thinking
"project"

Projects are the mechanism by which organizations and individuals change and adapt to take advantage of new opportunities or to counter threats. In a world in which business competitiveness is based on a search for new products and ways to do things, we can all improve our prospects by thinking: "Where is the project in my current situation?"

01

What is a project?

A project is a piece of work that is designed to bring about an agreed beneficial change within a fixed time frame using specified resources. Projects usually require the coordinated activity of a number of people to achieve that outcome, and often incorporate an element of risk. The projects in this book focus on change in organizations, and run for a defined length of time alongside the day-to-day work of an organization.

What makes a task a project?

Projects are the way in which human creativity is most effectively harnessed to achieve tangible, lasting results. In the past they may have been called something different, but building a pyramid, painting a ceiling, or founding a nation all required vision, planning, and coordinated effort—the essential features of what we now call a project. In practical terms, just about any initiative or piece of work that is too large or unfamiliar to be completed successfully without some measure of preparation and planning can, and usually should, be approached as a project.

Vision, planning, and coordinated effort—the essential features of a **project**

97% of organizations believe that **project management** is critical for **good performance** and **success**

A project is a "one-off" **scope of work** defined by three parameters— **time, cost, and quality**

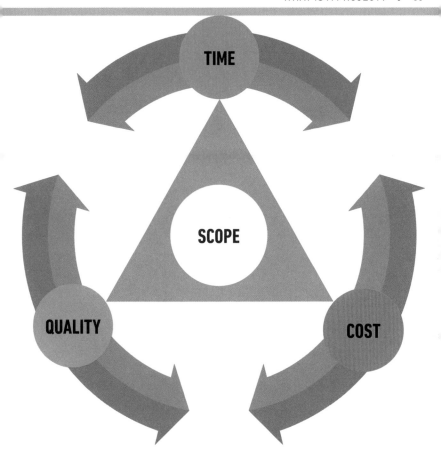

Defining a project

At its simplest level, a project is a "one-off" scope of work defined by three parameters—time, cost, and quality. In other words, it is the means by which a particular result is delivered using specified resources within a set period of time.

For most projects, one of these three parameters is "fixed" (i.e. should not or cannot change), but there is flexibility in at least one of the other two. Where the quality of the product is fixed (bringing a new drug to market, for example), costs have a tendency to rise and deadlines to slip if work is more extensive or complex than was first envisaged. Where the deadline is fixed (as for a tender deadline or a business conference), people either throw more resources at the project to make sure that it is ready on time, or they cull desirable but nonessential features in order to deliver the essential elements of quality within the time frame available.

Achieving change

Some projects are highly visible—large building projects, for example—while for others, only those directly involved will have any understanding of, or interest in, what they will deliver. Whatever the size and nature of a project, the main aim is always to bring about a change that is viewed as beneficial by whoever is sponsoring it. Many organizations use project management systems and methods to implement change. These include CPM (Critical Path Method), PERT (Program Evaluation and Review Technique), PRINCE 2 (PRojects IN Controlled Environments), and Agile (see pp.17). Some were devised for specific industries but have become widespread. All have their pros and cons, and suit certain types of project more than others.

The **Eden Project** has been visited by more than **22 million people**

Case study

SETTING THE STANDARD

When Sir Tim Smit pitched the idea of creating a science-based visitor attraction showcasing 100,000 plants from around the world in a disused clay pit in southwest England, few would have expected the Eden Project to have become the icon it is today. Despite the many technological challenges of creating the world's largest greenhouses—two giant transparent domes—the main construction phase was complete by March 2001. Since then, it has been visited by more than 22 million people at a rate of over one million a year, and has brought hundreds of millions of dollars to the local economy. Eden is now a significant contributor to the global debate on sustainable development and environmental issues, and is building on its experience to create a host of sister projects around the world. Commentators offer a variety of explanations for its success: technology made the original design and spectacular scale possible, but Smit's vision, inspirational leadership, and refusal to compromise on quality were undoubtedly central.

O **January 1995:** Sir Tim Smit has the idea for creating a huge site displaying the world's most important plants. **In October 1996,** architects sketch initial plans based on the shape of giant bubbles.

O **October 1998:** rains disrupt the first months of construction; the project devises a special drainage system. In **March 2000** Eden gains the 50% public match-funding promised in 1997.

O **March 2001:** the Eden Project opens to visitors and by **July 2008,** the ten millionth visitor arrives and is greeted by Tim Smit in person.

O **July 2017:** Eden Project International launches. As well as sites in Australia and China, future Edens are set to include the mussel-shell-shaped Eden Project North in Morecambe, UK, due to open in 2024.

The project sequence

The lifecycle of any project consists of six main phases: initiation, definition, planning, control, implementation, and review. At whichever point you, as project manager, enter the project's life, be sure to acquaint yourself as fully as possible with any preceding phases you have missed.

Defining project phases

The first phases of the project should lead to a clear outline of the overall parameters of time, cost, and quality. These factors form the scope of your project (see p.11).

   The initiation and definition phases involve using tools and approaches to identify the situation to be addressed, the desired end result, and the core team responsible for making it happen. Once these are established, the planning phase focuses on the detail of what has to be produced and how this can be done most effectively with minimum risk. At this stage, schedules and budgets should be finalized and the elements of risks and benefits should be added to the scope of the project.

The six phases of a project:

01 | **INITIATION**

02 | **DEFINITION**

03 | **PLANNING**

04 | **CONTROL**

05 | **IMPLEMENTATION**

06 | **REVIEW**

Tip

FOCUS ON DEFINITION
Fully explore the **"whats"** and **"whys"** of the project before you start to make **practical plans**—this will help you avoid the need for costly revisions in later phases.

Scope and overlap

The project's scope describes the desired end result of a project. Scope often includes reference to the context in which the end result of the project will be delivered, and who the end user will be. There is some overlap between project phases, especially at the start, and planning continues throughout the project. Generally, there comes a point at which significant resources are committed, and the control phase sees work begin.

The **planning phase** focuses on the **detail** of what has to be **produced** and how this can be done most **effectively** with **minimum risk**

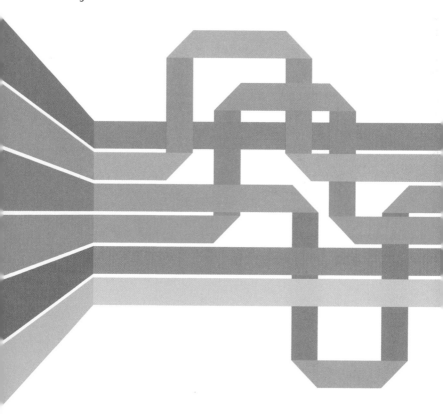

Controlling and implementing

The schedules and budgets that you established while planning will allow you to track progress and make adjustments as needed. As the control phase nears completion, focus switches to preparation for the moment when the results will "go live." While you should have been considering the needs and expectations of end users at every stage, your primary focus during this implementation phase should be taking steps to ensure that they react positively to the change your project has brought about. Plan your review stage around predefined criteria by which the project's success can be measured. These can then be used to declare it complete before moving into a phase where resources are reallocated and lessons learned.

Maintaining flexibility

While in theory the phases supply a logical sequence, in practice they often overlap, so you must adopt a process of continuous review during the definition, planning, and control phases. You may need to modify the scope (see p.11) to fit with what proves to be possible once you have an initial plan. Similarly, experience gained early on may help you identify flawed assumptions about the duration of tasks, leading you to reevaluate time frames, budgets, and other resources.

The six phases of a project:

INITIATION

DEFINITION

PLANNING

CONTROL

IMPLEMENTATION

REVIEW

77% of **high-performing** US organizations understand the **value** of project management

In focus

WATERFALL VS. AGILE

The six-phase method outlined here and throughout this book represents the "waterfall" model, in which each phase linearly follows the next. While this method suits a vast array of project types, other more flexible, "cyclical" models, such as Agile—whereby projects are broken up and developed portion by portion in short "sprints" lasting just a few weeks each—can work better in certain cases, especially in complex software development projects. While much of the advice in this book applies equally to Agile projects, Agile differs in following each phase multiple times, rather than just once. Each Agile sprint is a mini-project in its own right, in which one self-contained part is planned, designed, implemented, and tested in close collaboration with the client/end user. This allows greater adaptability—useful when project goals are hard to define clearly at the outset—but also makes it more complex, requiring a committed, experienced, and disciplined team to run it.

Identifying the problem to be solved or **opportunity** to be exploited.

Refining your **understanding** of what you want **to achieve,** by when, and with what resources.

Deciding in detail how to achieve **the objective**—time frames, resources, responsibilities, and communications.

Doing the work, monitoring progress, and **adjusting the plan** according to need.

Passing what you have **created** over to those who will be using it, and **helping them to adjust** to any changes.

Assessing the outcome and looking back to see if there is anything you could have done differently or better.

Defining the team

Role clarity is essential if you are to deliver a successful project, as every project is a new and often unique scope of work, and project teams are often built from scratch. Each stakeholder—a person who has influence over, or interest in, the process or outcome of the project—should be clear about exactly what the role entails and what should be delivered.

Understanding key roles

Every project is different, but there are a number of key roles that apply to most projects (see below). The relationship between these roles is functional rather than hierarchical. Although by the nature of the role the sponsor will usually be the most senior member of the project team—and will certainly be more senior than the manager—little else can be assumed about the relative seniority of other members of the team. Technical specialists, in particular, often have skills based on years of experience and are often "senior" to the project manager.

Key project roles

MANAGER

Has day-to-day responsibility for the project at executive level. Manager and sponsor must be **in complete agreement** about what constitutes **success** with respect to time, cost, and quality.

SPONSOR

The person who owns and controls the resources needed for the **project's success** and on whose **authority** the project rests.

CLIENT (OR SENIOR USER)

Coordinates or **represents the interests** and needs of the end-user group. If there are many end-user groups, each with differing views, there may be multiple clients.

Tip

BEWARE THE BUYER
Buyers often **wield significant power** when a project has been procured. Those who also act as the client can sometimes have an adversarial relationship with the project. Handle such clients carefully, using the sponsor where necessary.

Knowing your team

Your project team will generally be made up of people from within your organization and outside contractors. These people are key stakeholders in your project's success, so as project manager their motivation and focus is your priority. This may take skill and effort: team members often have other work to juggle and will be influenced by a second ring of stakeholders over whom you have no direct control (or know nothing about), such as line managers, colleagues, and suppliers. If they work remotely, it may take even more time and effort to forge trust, communicate a clear vision, and keep everyone aligned.

QUALITY ASSURANCE
In larger projects, a separate team may be assigned to **ensure** that all the prescribed methodologies are **carried out properly.** (In many smaller projects, the sponsor should do this.)

TECHNICAL SPECIALISTS
In many projects, success depends on the input of a small number of people with **expert essential skills,** high levels of crucial access, or personal decision-making authority.

BUYER
Buyers procure or **commission projects** on behalf of end users, and they are judged primarily on their ability to source reliable suppliers and **negotiate** competitive rates on contracts.

END USERS
Often, end users are **represented** by the client, but there are key points in most projects when it is **helpful to communicate** directly with this group.

Being project manager

As a project manager, you will be the central hub around which your project team is formed. Much of your success will depend on your ability to make the project something others want to be involved in or, at the very least, do not want to oppose.

Owning the project

Whether you have been delegated the role of project manager, or you sold an idea upward to someone capable of sponsoring it, you are likely to have demonstrated personal and managerial competence and commitment to the change under consideration.

"Competence" and "commitment" are the sorts of solid but colorless words often found in management books. However, the last thing a project manager can afford to be is colorless. In fact, the best project managers are a paradoxical combination of "larger than life"—self-confident, decisive, creative, and engaging—and self-effacing: down to earth, hands on, and keen to learn from other members of their team and promote their contributions.

Success comes from building diverse individuals into a **strong team** and **motivating** them to produce **quality results** within the requisite **timeframes**

Selling the idea

To be fully convincing as a project manager, you must first be convinced of the value of the initiative under consideration yourself. If you do not believe the results are attainable, or are lukewarm about their value, you are unlikely to make the sacrifices or identify the creative solutions required when the going gets tough—as it almost invariably will at some point. Furthermore, you must be able to communicate your enthusiasm to others and have the confidence to stand up to opposition both inside and outside the project team. Conversely, you must be a good listener—able to sift through the opinions of others and take on their ideas whenever they improve the quality of outcome or the likelihood of success.

> ### Tip
>
> **PLAY DEVIL'S ADVOCATE**
> Anticipate opposition by thinking through possible criticisms of your project and coming up with **effective** counterarguments so that you are **well prepared** to tackle negative views.

Taking on responsibility

To be an effective project manager, you must have a balance of task- and people-related skills. While your ultimate aim is to deliver a result, success comes from building diverse individuals into a strong team and motivating them to produce quality results within the requisite timeframes. Often, you will achieve this through personal determination, creativity, and powers of persuasion. At a deeper level, you also need the moral courage and integrity to treat every member of the team the same, irrespective of their seniority, personality, and location (whether in your office or working remotely). You also need excellent time management and personal organization, so that you can think beyond immediate distractions or crises to provide proactive leadership to other members of the team. While it is important to have at least some understanding of the technical aspects, your management role is to provide the decision-making, planning, and leadership skills outlined in this book.

CHECKLIST...

Am I ready to manage this project?

		YES	NO
1	Do I have a **clear idea** of who the end users are in my project and what the world looks like through their eyes?	☐	☐
2	Do I **understand what is required** of this project and why?	☐	☐
3	Do I **care about the outcome** enough to make personal sacrifices to achieve it?	☐	☐
4	Am I **confident I can deliver** it, given the constraints of cost and time?	☐	☐
5	Am I **prepared to take risks** and back my own judgment where necessary?	☐	☐

Working with your sponsor

The relationship between the project manager and the sponsor is the foundation upon which the whole project is built. Both must have the same understanding of what constitutes success and should have established a relationship of trust that enables each to share issues and concerns with the other as soon as they crop up.

Engaging the sponsor

Your sponsor should be the individual (rather than the group, committee, or team) who owns the resources required to make the project successful and will act as the final arbiter of success. This will be based partly on hierarchical seniority and partly on personal authority. Effective sponsorship is one of the key determinants of your success, so a wise project manager invests time and effort, first in selecting the right person—if you have a choice; second in forging the right relationship; and third in providing the sponsor with the information and arguments he or she needs to defend or champion the project as necessary.

Meeting your sponsor

Your first meeting with the sponsor of your project is a key moment of influence. This meeting should not be just about the detail of the project, but it should also establish how you and the sponsor will work together to make the project succeed.

Give high priority to agreeing the communication channels and escalation procedures—these will outline how and when to involve the sponsor when things go wrong. In larger projects, key team members such as a senior user or technical specialist may also be invited to attend this initial meeting with the sponsor.

In focus

CHOOSING YOUR OWN PROJECT SPONSOR

If you are in a position to choose your sponsor, your goal should be to achieve just the right balance between authority and accessibility. While it is generally helpful to have as senior a sponsor as possible, you also need someone for whom the project is significant enough to command their active interest.

A sponsor who keeps up to date with your progress and is aware of potential or actual issues will be well placed to make decisions or help you overcome any opposition or obstacle to the project without the need for extensive briefing. You need to be able to consult your sponsor quickly when things go wrong and feel comfortable that you are more than just one commitment among many.

How to forge a good sponsor-manager relationship

Be clear on your own role: this will give the sponsor **confidence** that you are the **right person** for the job.

Find out from them what **information** is required, when or how frequently it is needed, and in what format.

Express **clear expectations** to ensure you set a worthwhile "contract" upon which to build your **relationship.**

Use examples and **scenarios** to agree how you should interact when things go wrong.

Take time to establish **personal rapport** with the sponsor.

Ask about your sponsor's past projects and project managers, to establish their **style** of working and **likes and dislikes.**

Identifying poor sponsorship

Beware the sponsor who cancels or postpones your meetings on short notice, or who fails to get your project on the agenda of key decision-making meetings. Quickness to apportion blame, or to get unnecessarily embroiled in detail, are other indications that your sponsor has become detached from the aims and progress of your project. Think very carefully about what you should do and who you might speak to if your sponsor's lack of engagement starts to threaten the success of your project.

Tip

AVOID SURPRISES
Never try to hide things that have gone wrong from **your sponsor**—even if this means admitting a serious mistake on your part.

Documenting progress

Standard documents and agreed circulation and sign-off procedures increase the efficiency of project teams and improve communication, particularly between sponsor and manager. If your organization does not yet have guidelines for digital or hard-copy project documents, you can enhance your reputation considerably by producing your own.

Designing documentation

One of the many advantages of using project management software or online collaboration apps (see pp.52–53) is that they help you organize your data and present it attractively. They are also customizable: make sure that any charts, reports, or other documents you create, especially if they will be carried over from one project milestone to the next—or even transferred from project to project—are clear and consistent. Never underestimate presentation: people are quick to judge based on first impressions, and if your output looks professional, they will treat you as such unless you subsequently prove otherwise.

Key documents

Ensure your project management app integrates data from key project documentation and allows you to manipulate it, if necessary. Depending on the nature of your project, this may include:

Tip

PROTECT DATA

Data breaches can be expensive and even lead to **legal action,** so keeping your documents **safe** is paramount. Make regular backups and ensure your team understands how breaches happen, how to **prevent** them, and follows agreed **security measures.**

Signing off documents

Document sign-off is a useful way to get people to take a project seriously, and most project management software allows you to do this digitally. If people are good at delivering on promises, sign-off may not be needed—be guided by your company culture. With external clients or where a firmer line is required, a sign-off policy is most easily achieved if you implement it from the start.

Your software will save the signed-off version along with previous versions for reference. If you are not using software and are storing documents on company servers or in the cloud, number each version manually.

INITIATION PHASE
Mandate: agreement of the need for the project and its aims.
Brief: a description of the issue to be resolved or the opportunity to be exploited.

01

DEFINITION PHASE
Project Initiation Document (PID): defines what the project must deliver and why.
Business case: the financial figures behind the opportunity.
Risk log: a record of all risks and approaches to resolution.

02

PLANNING PHASE
Schedule and resource plans: the plan in detail, including completion dates and resource requirements.
Quality plan: what processes will be monitored, and how.

03

CONTROL PHASE
Changes to scope: agreed modifications to the original brief.
Milestone reviews: progress against schedule and budget.
Quality reviews: confirmation that processes are being followed.

04

IMPLEMENTATION PHASE
User Acceptance Test (UAT): reports and sign-offs from end users at all levels.
Implementation schedule: the plan for how the project will be handed over to end users.

05

REVIEW PHASE
Post-implementation review: assesses what the project has delivered.
Lessons learnt review: how things could have been done better.

06

Setting up
a project

A successful project depends on clear thinking in the preparatory stages. The initiation and definition phases of the project management process build on each other to establish precisely what the project is expected to deliver to the end users, while the planning phase sets out how this is to be achieved.

02

Initiating the project

The aim of the initiation phase is to set out the reasons for a project and the context in which it will run. As project manager your aim in this phase is to secure the briefing, backing, and resources you need from your sponsor to begin a detailed evaluation of the work to be undertaken.

Agreeing on the brief

The first step in the initiation phase is to establish that both you and your sponsor view success in the same terms—both the result to be achieved and the way you will work together to achieve it. Based on these discussions the project mandate and brief can be drawn up. These should document, respectively, the business opportunity or issue to be addressed, and some outline thoughts on how this might best be done. The initiation phase should end with the sponsor signing off on the brief and allocating resources that allow you to move into the definition and planning phases of your project.

> Establish that both **you** and **your sponsor view success** in the **same terms**—both the **result** to be achieved and the way you will **work together**

Getting the right support

The type of support you need from your sponsor during this phase will, to a degree, be dependent on where the idea for the project originated.
● **Top-down initiation** In most organizations, targets for future development and plans for a variety of initiatives become projects undertaken by operational managers. In this kind of "top-down" initiation, the sponsor delegates the execution of the project to you. This is a critical point for you: do not let nerves or excitement cloud your judgement of what you need at this stage. You can expect strong support from above, but also need to secure a very clear brief of what is expected of the project.

62%
of projects have **actively engaged** executive sponsors

• **Bottom-up initiation** Not all the best ideas come from those at the top of an organization; those closest to the customer may be first to spot commercial opportunities. Successful projects initiated from the "bottom up," by people who end up managing them, indicate a very healthy corporate culture. It shows that those at more junior levels are having initiative rewarded with real responsibility—and this represents an opportunity that should be seized. Your advantage in this case is that you will be highly motivated, with a very clear idea of what you want to achieve and how this could be made possible. Your priority is to obtain solid support from a sponsor who is fully behind the project so that you can go on to deliver results that justify his or her confidence in you.

In focus

PITCHING YOUR OWN PROJECT
If you identify an opportunity requiring more resources than you personally can muster, your first step should be to target a suitable sponsor and pitch your idea. Your presentation should identify the size of the opportunity and be supported by hard evidence. Think about the questions your sponsor might ask. Prepare well: there are unknowns and risks in any project, so your sponsor's decision will be based as much on your credibility as the strength of the idea. Even if you do not get sponsorship for this idea, you can enhance your prospects of getting future projects sponsored if you present a well-argued case.

Your priority is to obtain **solid support** from a sponsor who is **fully behind the project**

Building a project team

One of the most important functions of a project manager is to build and maintain the "team dynamic." By giving your project a strong and positive identity, and creating a rewarding environment in which to work, you make it more likely that people will give you that "extra 10 percent" that dramatically increases the quality of their contribution and makes them easier to manage.

Putting a team together

An effective project manager builds a team with a strong sense of identity. This is often more challenging in small teams than in those with a high profile and fully dedicated members. Start by taking time to select the right people, with input from the sponsor (see pp.18–19). Base your decisions on availability and relevant skills/knowledge/contacts, but also take personality "fit" and motivation into account. Be aware that today's tech tools allow for much more seamless long-distance collaboration, so don't be afraid to cast a wide net. Stakeholder analysis (see pp.32–33) can be a useful tool for assessing potential candidates and finding the best way to manage them. Make a personal approach to each person selected and request their participation. Don't beg—simply explain why you have selected them and the benefits they can expect for getting involved.

Getting started

Hold an initial meeting with all project team members. It is helpful to have the sponsor present for a proportion of a "kickoff" meeting, but you will enhance your authority as the project manager if you are the one to arrange and chair the meeting. (If you lack the authority to do this, you may struggle to manage the group in the long run.) Discuss team roles and ground rules for your project before getting into the detail of the task to be undertaken. Find out if there is anything your team members particularly like or dislike about project teamwork, and what their hopes and concerns are. Talk with them about how project decisions (particularly in relation to deadlines) will be made; how the team will acknowledge success; what to do if people fail to deliver; and how conflicts will be resolved.

Make sure any remote team members feel just as involved: ensure they can attend the meeting virtually, get copies of any documents you distribute and, above all, have the opportunity to be heard.

Members of your team will take greater **"ownership"** of your project if they feel an **important part** of it

Developing identity

A strong team is built on a strong identity. Give your project a name, but beware of choosing anything too clever—the best names are generally low key, with positive connotations, offering a useful shorthand reference for the project. Create a team location, be it a building, room, desk, or notice board, or a virtual location on the intranet or web. Make it somewhere that information can be displayed and progress checked, and give people reasons to frequent it.

Select the **right people,** with input from the **sponsor**

Members of your team will take greater "ownership" of your project if they feel as if they are an important part of it. Involve them in production of the work schedule, risk analysis, and problem solving. Establish the "soft" success criteria, relating to teamwork, morale, personal behaviour, and learning, in addition to the hard criteria set out in your project definition.

CHECKLIST...
Creating a strong team

	YES	NO
1 Do **my team members** know one another?	☐	☐
2 Do they **respect** one another?	☐	☐
3 Do they know how **their roles** fit together?	☐	☐
4 Have they agreed **the standards** to which they will hold one another accountable?	☐	☐
5 Do they **acknowledge** my role as project manager?	☐	☐

Analyzing stakeholders

The various stakeholders in your project—from the sponsor to each individual internal team member—all view it from very different perspectives. Analysis of each stakeholder's attitude toward your project, and degree of influence within it, can be a useful part of the process by which a team is put together and managed.

Identifying key players

All projects have multiple stakeholders. Some will be more important than others, either because of their involvement in delivering elements of the work, or because they are influential in the environment where the work is being produced or will be deployed.

Stakeholder analysis allows you to identify the most important people in your project and decide where to invest time and resources. It should lead to a communication plan aimed initially at canvassing opinion and then providing the right people with timely information throughout the project's life cycle.

> **Stakeholder analysis** allows you to identify important people and decide where to invest **time** and **resources**

Performing the analysis

Consider every stakeholder in your project in relation to two scales—influence and attitude. Rate each person or group according to their influence within the project, and whether they can be influenced by you as the project manager. Next, rate them on their attitude toward the project. Use the matrix on the facing page to mark the desired and actual position of stakeholders. The blue figures show the current positions of stakeholders you wish were more committed, so consider what you need to do to improve the situation. The red figure is neutral, but is unlikely to be influenced by you, so does not require action.

INFLUENCE

Significant influence; cannot always be influenced by you

Marginal influence; cannot always be influenced by you

Influence equal to you

Significant influence; can be influenced by you

Marginal influence; can be influenced by you

ATTITUDE

Influencing stakeholders

As a general rule, you are unlikely to be able to move strongly negative stakeholders to the positive side, but it may be possible to neutralize their opposition. Where there is opposition from an especially powerful stakeholder or group of stakeholders, steps may have to be taken to reduce their influence or the project may have to be abandoned. Your relationship with the sponsor, and his or her position in your organization, may be very helpful. You need to have the confidence to address senior or challenging stakeholders directly, but also the wisdom to know when this may be counterproductive and a situation is better addressed by involving the sponsor.

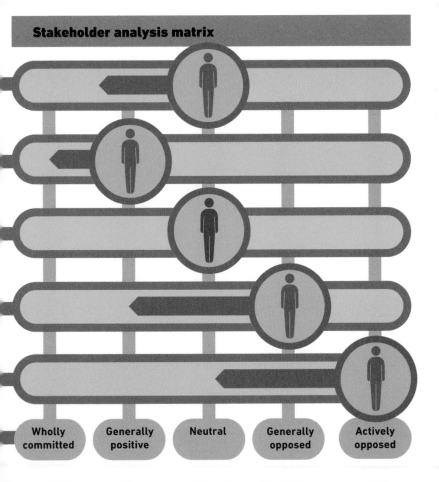

Stakeholder analysis matrix

| Wholly committed | Generally positive | Neutral | Generally opposed | Actively opposed |

Defining the details

Before committing significant resources, you must have agreement on what your project should produce, by when, and using what resources. While the brief should have identified the rationale and broad strategy behind a project, the next step is to define the scope of the project— precisely what will be handed over to the end users on completion.

Asking for input

In broad terms, defining the scope of your project is done by asking the right people the right questions in the right way, and recording your findings clearly. Consider the most important players in your project, identified in your stakeholder analysis: which of these have key roles in defining what the project must deliver? Time invested discussing the project brief with stakeholders, particularly the client and end users, is rarely wasted. The views of the sponsor are a good starting point—if your project required an initiation phase, you will have already obtained these from the mandate and the brief.

Tip

ASK "GREAT QUESTIONS"

Think carefully about the questions you ask your **client.** If you can get him or her to say **"That's a great question!"** you will have helped uncover a **new perspective,** and transformed your **status** from supplier to **partner.**

Speaking directly

Clients and end users should have significant input into the scope of your project, but also consider those people with whom they interact, such as anyone who manages the end users or who will support them in areas relating to your project after implementation. It may also be helpful to speak to anyone who will be responsible for maintaining the product, capability, or facility that your project will deliver.

92%

of **attendees value meetings** in which they can **contribute**

Defining the **scope** of your **project** is done by asking the **right people** the **right questions** in the **right way**

Time invested **discussing** the **project brief** with **stakeholders** is rarely wasted

Gathering information

Focused and well-structured conversations not only deliver useful information from stakeholders, but can also build your credibility with the client. Generally speaking, it is best to have these discussions face-to-face, or by video call, as this allows you to assess each person's understanding of, and commitment to, the project. Although your primary purpose is to uncover the information you need to create a clear scope, in-depth questioning often exposes hitherto unexplored aspects of people's work to scrutiny. This can sometimes be resented, so tread carefully, but be brave enough to continue lines of questioning that are uncovering useful information.

44%

of organizations are likely to **deliver** projects that meet their **original goal** and business intent

In-depth questioning often exposes hitherto unexplored aspects of people's work to scrutiny—**be courageous** enough to **continue lines of questioning** that are uncovering **useful information**

Understanding your client

Your first aim should be to establish how well your client understands the situation surrounding your project and the benefit they expect it to deliver. Inexperienced project managers sometimes make the mistake of trying to zero in too quickly on what the client sees as the essential and desirable features of the end product. In cases where the client does not know what they want, avoid asking direct questions about the scope, as this is likely to confuse and could lead to frustration, embarrassment, and conflict. This would not be the ideal start to a crucial relationship that should become a central axis of the project team.

Asking the right questions to define the scope

HOW?	O **How will** it be used? O **How long** will it be in service for?
WHERE?	O **Where will** it be used? Physically, and in what context? O **Where is** this in our list of priorities?
WHO?	O **Who are** the end users? O **Who will** support it? O **Who will** manage it?
WHEN?	O **When will** it be used?
WHY?	O **Why is** the result required? O **Why doesn't** it exist already?
WHAT?	O **What is** the problem to be fixed? O **What would** be the impact of not fixing it? O **What exactly** is the result required? O **What has** been tried before?

CHECKLIST...
Understanding the scope of your project

	YES	NO
1 Do you have a **clear idea** of the objective of your project— what it is intended to achieve?	☐	☐
2 Do you know why this is **important**?	☐	☐
3 Do you know how and when it will be **achieved**?	☐	☐
4 Have you **determined** who will be involved?	☐	☐
5 Have you **identified** the deliverables for your project?	☐	☐
6 Have you obtained enough **information** to allow your sponsor to make a **decision** on whether to proceed?	☐	☐

Prioritizing features
In most projects, as you go through the definition process you will identify a number of features required of the end result. Some will be essential, while others are "nice to have." In order to highlight where clashes exist, take each feature in turn and create designs based on that alone; then consider the results with the client and develop a definition that delivers the perfect mix of features to the end user.

> If the sequence of **questions** does not lead to one of your organization's **strategic goals** within **five steps**, the project may not be worth pursuing

Tip

CREATE A BOTTOM LINE
Set a "Fit for Purpose Baseline"— the minimum that your project can **deliver** and still be deemed a **success.**

Adding creativity

As part of the definition phase of your project, it is worth considering how it could be transformed from delivering a "fit for purpose" solution to being a project that catches the eye for creativity and elegance. This need not take much time; the main thing is to suspend judgment on ideas and have some fun. Then change your mindset and assess what additional perspectives your creative musings have uncovered. Try to identify more than one option—even when there is an obvious solution. Take time to consider at least three possible approaches (one of these might be "do nothing"). Your aim should be to find one way to make your project exciting and different for your end users or your team.

Recording the scope

The investigations you undertake during the definition phase are to enable you to generate a detailed Project Information Document (PID). This is an expansion of the brief, incorporating all the additional information you have gathered from discussions with stakeholders. The PID is the document on which the sponsor will make a decision on whether to commit significant resources to the project. Once signed off, it becomes a binding agreement between the sponsor, the project manager, and the client, so its format and content are of paramount importance. The information in the PID needs to be easily accessible, so don't include more than is necessary for the size and complexity of your project.

THE FIVE WHYS

A simple but surprisingly powerful technique for establishing the link between a project and your organization's key strategic objectives is to ask the client why they want what the project delivers. Insist that they answer this question beginning with the words "in order to." Then take the answer they give and ask them why that is important; again, insist on "in order to." Repeat this process for as many times as it takes to connect your project to your organization's main business strategy. As a rule of thumb, if the sequence of questioning does not lead to one of your organization's strategic goals within five steps, then the project may not be worth pursuing.

Developing a business case

Every project will represent an investment in time, effort, and resources, so a key question to address during the definition phase is: "Is this project worth it?" The business case for a project weighs two factors: the cost of undertaking the project and the benefits it is likely to deliver.

Weighing costs

When assessing the potential costs of your project, make sure you only take future costs into account—past expenditures are irrelevant in deciding whether to take the project forward. Only include incremental costs in your assessment: those that change as a result of the project being undertaken. For example, if your project requires that you hire two extra staff but is running from company offices, the additional staff costs should be included but the accommodation costs should not. Your assessment should include any costs relating to the involvement of your internal team—often known as an invisible cost, as no money changes hands—and out-of-pocket costs, which are those that will be paid outside your organization, such as the cost of materials or subcontracted services.

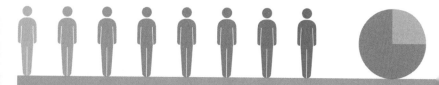

66%

of organizations **do not** regularly complete projects **on budget**

GETTING THE BUSINESS CASE RIGHT

Dos	Don'ts
O **Using the sponsor's financial advisors to put together your business case**	O Basing your business case on your own gut feelings and untested assumptions
O **Setting a notional hourly rate for work done by internal team members, especially technical specialists**	O Considering internal team costs a "free" resource when additional or unplanned work has to be done
O **Including contingency funds in your cost assessment, to allow for unexpected outlays**	O Deciding to ignore potential risks and take the chance that nothing will go wrong

Tip

KNOW YOUR STUFF
Work with **experts** to put your **business case** together, but make sure you understand the basis on which they have done this well enough to **form a view** on what they have produced.

Assessing benefits

While it is often easy to identify the "change" your project will deliver, it may be more difficult to quantify the nature, scale, and timing of the benefit. As a rule, the benefits from a project should be aligned with at least one of the organization's strategic goals (such as increasing revenue or reducing costs, for example) if it is to proceed. Consider also the point at which the benefits can be expected. In some cases, a smaller return earlier is preferable to a larger one that will take longer to come in.

Rarely can projected benefits be guaranteed, so any complete cost/benefit analysis should contain an assessment of what could go wrong and the effect of this on the overall outcome. While your aim should be to put a percentage figure on the likelihood for the project delivering the intended benefit, this is always a judgment based on incomplete information. In the end it is your sponsor's job to make the decision, but it must be based on accurate information provided by you.

Managing risk

Projects, by their nature, are risky, so it could therefore be argued that your key role as a project manager is to identify, plan for, and manage risk. Risk analysis is undertaken in the definition phase, but should be followed by a continuous cycle of management and analysis throughout the control and implementation phases of your project.

Planning for risk

Initial identification of risk often takes the form of a Risk Workshop—a group of people getting together with the express intention of identifying and evaluating all the risks in a particular project or phase. From that point on every review meeting should contain an agenda item on "open" or "live" risks. As a project manager, the risks you should be most concerned with are those that will have an impact on one of the three project parameters (time, cost, or quality).

Risks need to be evaluated with respect to two criteria: probability (how likely they are to happen) and impact (how serious it would be if they do). Most tasks will contain some element of risk, so you will need to set a threshold at which you are going to begin to plan.

Dealing with risk

These are the five ways of dealing with risk, as outlined in the international project management standard PRINCE2 (see p.12).

Recording risk

For tasks that carry a risk that is above your threshold for probability and impact, identify a response in advance, and monitor progress toward project completion more carefully than usual.

In all but the smallest projects, risks should be recorded in a risk log. This document describes each risk, its impact and probability, and countermeasures to deal with it. It can also include the proximity of the risk (when it will need active management) and any early indicators that the probability of the risk has changed. The contents of the risk log should be reviewed throughout the life cycle of the project.

64%

of project managers
usually undertake
risk management

PLAN CONTINGENCY

Have a **Plan B** that will achieve the same **result** by a different route and leave future plans intact.

PREVENT

Terminate the risk by **doing things differently.** This is not always a realistic possibility.

REDUCE

Take action to reduce either the likelihood or impact of the risk.

TRANSFER

See if you can **spread the risk** so that the consequences become less serious (this is the principle on which insurance works).

ACCEPT

There are some risks that are considered **acceptable** because the cost of dealing with them is **greater** than the **increased benefit** one would get from having to develop countermeasures.

Risks need to be **evaluated** with respect to **two criteria:** probability and impact

Planning the project

The production of an accurate and detailed plan is one of the project manager's most important responsibilities. However, do not make the mistake of thinking you should do it on your own. By involving the team in the planning process you increase their understanding of what has to be done and generally gain an extra level of commitment to deadlines.

Developing a project plan

The following ten-step Team Planning technique uses a virtual whiteboard app (or an analogue flip chart and sticky notes) to produce a project plan. By following the process outlined, you will produce a robust and accurate project plan and maximize buy-in from those who will be instrumental in delivering it. Do the first four steps on your own, getting the team involved once you have some raw material for them to work on. This reduces the cost of planning and makes briefing easier, as you have something to show them.

|01

Restate the objective

Start by reducing **the objective** of your project—defined in the **initiation and definition** process—into a single statement of intent that fits on one large sticky note.

Tip

PLANNING REMOTELY
Virtual whiteboard tools are ideal for planning meetings, especially for teams with remote workers, allowing everyone to add "sticky notes" and agree with comments. Examples include Miro, Bluescape, InVision, JamBoard, and Lucidspark.

|02
Brainstorm the products

The products of a plan are the **building blocks** that, when added together, **deliver** that project's **end result.** Brainstorm between five and 15 products for your project on separate sticky notes, placing them in roughly chronological order down the side of your whiteboard.

|03
Brainstorm the tasks

Tasks are **activities or actions** undertaken by individuals or groups that normally require their presence or participation for the whole duration. **Brainstorm the tasks** that need to be done by you and other people to deliver each of the products, writing one task on one sticky note—it's a good idea to choose a different color of note from the ones you wrote the products on. Draw two fields on the bottom half of the sticky note, so that you can add extra information later.

|04
Place the tasks in order

Place the tasks in roughly **chronological order** across the page, keeping them in line with the product to which they are connected. Where tasks can be done **simultaneously,** place them below one another, and where they depend on one another or on using the same resources, place them **sequentially.** Involve the rest of the delivery team in adding to and **refining** this skeleton plan.

32%

of the reasons for **project failure**
rest in **poor estimation** in the
planning phase

|05

Confirm the tasks

Step back and look at
the **logic flow** of your
plan. Involve the
implementation team in
this step—it can be a
useful **"reality check"**
on your logic. When
people **identify**
modifications to your
plan, listen carefully
and **incorporate their
suggestions,** changing
or adding sticky notes
as necessary.

|06

Draw in dependencies between tasks

A dependency is the
**relationship between
two tasks.** The most
common type of
dependency is **end–start**
(one task ending before
the next can start).
Dependency can be
based either on logic or
on resource. Once you
have confirmed all tasks
are represented and that
they are in the right
places, draw arrows
to represent the
dependencies between
the tasks required to
complete your project.

|07

Allocate times to tasks

Use the experience of
your project team to
identify what resources
and how much effort will
be required to complete
each task. Note: this is
not how long people
need to complete the
task ("Calendar time"),
but how much effort
will need to be put in
("Time-sheet time").
Write the time needed
for each task into the
bottom right-hand field
on each sticky note.
Where possible, use
the same unit of
time throughout.

Once you have confirmed **all tasks are represented** and that they are in the right places, **draw arrows** to represent the **dependencies between the tasks**

|08

Assess and resolve risks

Get **input** from every member of the project team on what they **consider** to be risks. Instruct each member of the team to place a comment or tag on the two or three tasks they consider riskiest. Once everyone has placed their comments, **facilitate a discussion** around their choices, **agreeing** what countermeasures to adopt and who will be responsible for them.

|09

Allocate tasks

Get your team together and **allocate who will do what.** People who have been allowed to contribute to the plan in the ways described in steps five to eight will generally have already identified the tasks they would **like to work on,** or at least recognized that they are the **best person** to do certain tasks even if they don't want to do them. Simply **introduce this step** by saying to your team: "Ok, who's going to do what?" and then wait for a response. You may be greeted with silence at first, but gradually people will begin to volunteer for tasks. Record names or initials in the bottom left-hand corner of each sticky note.

|10

Agree milestones and review points

Place one sticky note (the same color as those used for your project's products) at the end of each line of tasks. Now facilitate a **discussion** about when people will be able to complete their tasks and write specific dates (and possibly even times) for when you will **review progress.** If your project is time-critical, begin with the deadline and work back toward the present; if quality or cost are critical, begin at the present and work forward. Make sure that people cross-check their deadlines with other work or life commitments.

Example of a project plan

In this example, the project is to create a report containing the necessary information for a marketing director to allocate her budget for the coming year. It contains three main stages, and a number of smaller steps that need to take place within this framework. As is often the case in projects, various processes need to take place concurrently as well as consecutively.

PROJECT OBJECTIVE
Total time: 32 hours

Deliver: market analysis plus recommendations

To: marketing director

In order to: allow her to decide how to spend next year's budget

INTERNAL REVIEW UNDERTAKEN

Meet with marketing director to confirm strategic priorities	
Alan	4 hours

Conduct desk research	
Alan, Ali	8 hours

MARKET RESEARCH CONDUCTED

Select market research agency	
Priya	5 hours

REPORT PRODUCED

Write background section of report	
Alan	4 hours

34%

of organizations **mostly or always** complete projects **on time**

Conduct market research

Agency	2 weeks (lapsed time)

Analyze market-research findings and decide on key recommendations

Alan, Ali, Priya	6 hours

Write final draft report and prepare presentation

Alan	4 hours

Present to marketing director

Alan, Ali	1 hour

Estimating time

Being able to estimate the amount of time required for the tasks and activities of a project is a key skill for any project manager. Indeed, in smaller projects that do not have an explicit budget, keeping to time is likely to be one of the measures of your effectiveness as project manager.

Getting schedules right

In most cases, estimating task times with any degree of accuracy requires a combination of experience and common sense. However, this presupposes that you have correctly identified the task. When projects are late, it is often because activities have not been thought through or recorded properly, so what seemed like a very straightforward task (such as getting a decision from the finance department, for example) gets estimated as a single event rather than a number of small but significant and connected steps, each taking time and effort.

Involving the team

In most small projects, and certainly where many projects run side by side, the challenge is not to estimate how much effort tasks will take, but how much time someone needs to complete a task alongside their other work. Involve team members who will be performing critical tasks in your decision-making process. Ask each person for their estimation of the amount of time they will need to be able to complete a certain task, given their other commitments. Be prepared to challenge these estimates if you disagree, but beware of putting undue pressure on people to reduce them.

How to estimate the time required

Break down tasks until you know precisely who is doing what.

Ask people how long it will take to carry out their tasks.

Seek advice from those who have done similar tasks before.

Use a time estimation formula.

Using time estimation formulae

Different organizations, industries, and sectors employ different models or formulae to estimate time. At first sight they always seem mathematical, but in most cases their effectiveness is psychological—either overcoming aversion to estimating, or encouraging more careful thought in those who tend to rush in.

Perhaps the most widely known is the PERT formula (Project Evaluation and Review Technique). To use PERT you need three estimates of the time it could take to complete a task or activity:

- The most likely time required (Tm)
- The most optimistic time assessment (To)
- The most pessimistic time assessment (Tp)

Use the following formula to estimate the most probable duration for that activity (Te):

$$Te = \frac{To + 4Tm + Tp}{6}$$

The formula can be weighted toward pessimism—if the consequences of a late completion of a particular task are severe, for example—by reducing the Tm multiplier and adding a Tp multiplier:

$$Te = \frac{To + 3Tm + 2Tp}{6}$$

Representing the plan

Once created, your project plan should become your main point of reference for managing progress during the control phase of the project. It is a living document, and expect it to go through several iterations to keep up with changing circumstances and to take account of incorrect estimates of time or cost.

Finding the right system

Once you have developed your project plan, you will have a better idea of the kind of project-management software you need. There are many types available, each with its own strengths and weaknesses. Choosing the right tool or tools depends on the size and complexity of your project, and how your team will be collaborating. Some online software is weighted toward constant communication, with chat channels and video calling—useful when close collaboration is key; other types provide sophisticated tools for document management or workflow automation.

If your project requires you to compare multiple plans, calculate the impact of changes, or test variances, invest in specialist project management software that will do this automatically.

Also consider compatibility with the documents your team already uses day-to-day and where these are stored— whether in the cloud or on the company network. Finally, think about the user experience: go for something intuitive to use if stakeholders only need occasional access, and make sure the system you select isn't so complex that it gets in the way of managing the project itself.

ASK YOURSELF...
What are my requirements?

		YES	NO
1	What **aspects** of the plan will I need to **analyze** and when?	☐	☐
2	In what circumstances will I need to **present or discuss** the plan?	☐	☐
3	How often will it need **updating?**	☐	☐
4	Who else needs to have **access** to the plan?	☐	☐
5	Have you **identified** the deliverables for your project?	☐	☐
6	What representation will be most **easily accessible** and **understood** by the team?	☐	☐

Choosing software

SOFTWARE PACKAGE TYPE	STRENGTHS	WEAKNESSES
Specialist project management software Ideal for a niche project environment where people are familiar with its use and can intuitively read all formats and representations. Examples: LiquidPlanner, Wrike, Monday.com	O **Robust feature set** for heavyweight project management O Shows **dependencies** between tasks O **Integrates** schedule, budget, and resource plans O **Calculates** critical path and resources	O "Occasional" project managers may find interfaces **complicated** O Too sophisticated for small projects O Does not readily integrate project and **day-to-day work** O Can be **expensive**
Online collaboration tools Useful for simpler, smaller projects where communication, integration with day-to-day work, and budget are key considerations. Examples: Asana, Trello, Microsoft Teams, Slack	O Many features to support **remote team working** O **Clean, convenient** interfaces O Flexible and relatively easy to **customize** O Some are tablet or **smartphone-friendly**	O May not be powerful enough for highly **complex** projects O Project management features may require app **integration** O If you outgrow the free basic tier, **premium plans** can be expensive O Some lack **time-tracking** and reporting tools
Regular office software Your day-to-day suite of office tools or a simple cloud-based app may meet your needs. Examples: Microsoft Office 365, Google Workspace	O Widely available and **familiar to project stakeholders** O **Flexible** for smaller projects O **Spreadsheets** allow calculation of durations and costs O Ideal for **small projects** with no cash budget	O Requires **specialist knowledge** to represent more complex information (such as showing the relationships between tasks graphically) O Not good at showing **critical path**, resource plans, or budgets O Few, if any, **social functions** for remote working

Managing work
in progress

Management during the control phase, once a project is underway, requires a sophisticated skill set that includes team leadership, delegation and communication, budget and schedule management, and high performance under pressure.

03

Making time for the project

Project management is rarely a full-time role, except in large or specialist organizations. Finding time for longer-term work is often one of the biggest challenges faced by managers of smaller projects, especially when the planning stage ends and hands-on work begins.

Recognizing your priorities

Most modern approaches to time management address our tendency to prioritize urgency over importance when deciding what to do on a day-to-day basis. While the ability to react to unforeseen events and problems is essential, being purely "reactive" damages productivity, reduces the quality of results, and not least is stressful for you.

As a project manager your focus has to be further ahead than the immediate; hence the emphasis on definition and planning, on proactive communication with all stakeholders, and on risk analysis.

> **Tip**
>
> **TRACK YOUR TIME**
> Online calendars and to-do list apps are useful digital tools for organizing your team's and your own time. But for added insight, consider a dedicated time-management app such as RescueTime or Toggl Track, which tracks your computer activity and analyzes productivity.

CHECKLIST...
Managing your time   YES   NO

1 Do you allocate **"interruption-free"** time in your calendar, when you get away from your desk and turn off your email and phone, for tasks that require uninterrupted thought? .... ☐ ☐

2 Do you **factor reactive time**—spent responding to emails and phone calls and attending ad-hoc meetings—into your **day-to-day** planning? .... ☐ ☐

3 Do you discourage reactive **requests**? .... ☐ ☐

4 Do you **delegate** work early and **effectively**? .... ☐ ☐

5 Do you ensure, where possible, that meetings begin **on time** and stick to the **agenda**? .... ☐ ☐

Finding your focus

Finding time to focus on the big picture is the key to integrating your long-term role and responsibilities with the short-term demands of your project.

● Start with a plan: begin every day by spending five to ten minutes getting a handle on your agenda for that day. Identify time already allocated to meetings and other fixed tasks. Allocate time to the tasks you plan to do off your "to do" list. Plan in enough flexibility to deal with the unexpected, and at least one review point at which you can check your direction and make adjustments.

● Integrate project tasks with your day-to-day tasks and calendar. Do this by recording them on the same list and ensuring they are broken down to around the same size. If the average task size on your "to do" list is 15–30 minutes, for example, don't have project tasks of four hours in length—they won't get done.

● Motivate yourself to do longer-term tasks every day. Set yourself a goal of doing one longer-term task per day on each of your projects, or one task preparing for the next deliverable (i.e., not the current one) on every project.

Begin every day by **spending five to ten minutes** getting a handle on **your agenda** for that day

Delegating effectively

Set time aside on a regular basis to plan which tasks and activities can be delegated to others. This may not be restricted to project tasks: in order to have the time for project management, you may find that you have to delegate other parts of your job, too.

Getting delegation right

Successful delegation is not always easy, especially if you are managing a small project within a multi-project environment. As the manager of a small project you can expect to find yourself delegating longer-term tasks to busy people who may only have partial understanding of what you are trying to achieve, and for whom your project is a relatively low priority. When deciding which tasks and activities to delegate, take time to consider the benefits you could expect from delegating a particular task, and the blocks that you would need to overcome. Once you have identified potential opportunities for delegation, clarify the specifics of how you could achieve them by asking yourself:

- What is the required outcome or deliverable from delegating this task?
- Why is this important?
- How will it be used and when is it required by?
- What constraints are there on how the result can be achieved?
- What could go wrong?
- To whom should I delegate this task?
- Why should they do it?
- What objections might I need to overcome?
- What help will they need?
- What level of authority can they handle?

Overcoming barriers to delegation

GET EXPERIENCE

The best way to learn how to delegate is to have someone who **delegates effectively** to you. Note the attitudes and behaviors that overcome or bypass resistance, and use them when you delegate.

Take time to consider the **benefits** you could expect from **delegating a particular task**, and the blocks that you would need to overcome

BEAT INDECISION

Try to make **quick decisions** as to whom to approach and what precisely has to be done, and don't procrastinate about approaching the sponsor if their involvement is required.

FIGHT GUILT

Nice people don't like delegating unpleasant tasks. However, most **effective leadership** requires a hard head as well as a soft heart.

PLAN WELL

Think ahead, so you don't discover tasks that have to be done when it is too late to ask anyone else to do them.

80%

of employees **experience burnout** on the job at least **sometimes**

TACKLE FEAR

Fight any feelings that **delegated tasks** will not be done properly or on time, that your delegation request will be rejected, or that you will be shown up by someone doing a job better than you.

Preparing to delegate

Where possible, delegate straight from the plan: as soon as you have identified a task that needs to be done, select someone to do it. If they are present when the task is identified, use that moment to pass responsibility to them. Give delegatees as much warning as possible: it is preferable to have three weeks' warning of a deadline, rather than three days. Warn people of impending delegation, even before you are clear on what you want done. Brevity is of the essence and it's not a bad idea to use a standard format for this "heads-up message" (see left).

How to compose a heads-up message

DEFINE THE SCOPE OF THE TASK
Give a general description of the task to be delegated, e.g. "I've got some figures I need you to analyze."

SET A TIMEFRAME
Describe when work is likely to start and when it will be needed, e.g. "I will brief you on Monday for a deadline on Friday. The task should take about four hours."

ASK THE DELEGATEE TO PREPARE
Let the person know what they can be doing to prepare themselves for the work, e.g. "Can you set aside that amount of time next week?"

SET A MEETING DATE
Give a time and a place for a delegation meeting, e.g. "Let's set up a video call for Monday at 10am. Please check your diary."

Setting the details

Arrange a formal meeting to describe the details and parameters of the task to the delegatee. It is vital to the success of the task that your colleague has fully understood and is committed to what they have been asked to do. Ask open questions, such as, "How do you plan to do this?" This will give you a good idea about their level of understanding, but it can be quite challenging for the delegatee to answer without time to reflect.

Part one Describe what is required, by when, at what cost; why it is required; the context of what is required, including any restrictions on methods. By giving people entire jobs or the context of the job you will increase their motivation and understanding leading to a good result.

In focus

GIVING FEEDBACK
Longer-term delegation benefits greatly from formal (diarized) review and follow-up sessions. Follow the adage: "People don't do what you expect—they do what you inspect!" Ad-hoc checking is generally sloppy and inefficient—in fact, imprecise questions such as, "How are things going?" result in inexact answers, such as, "Oh, fine!," and almost invariably lead to problems at completion with missed deadlines or partial delivery. When reviewing work, accept what is good enough, don't criticize irrelevant details. Accept that a task may have been done differently than how you would have done it.

Holding a split meeting
Organize your delegation meeting in two parts with a "gap" to give the delegatee time to reflect before explaining how they will approach their task:

Gap Give your colleague time for reflection alone. Create the gap with a statement such as, "Let me get us a cup of coffee while you stay here and have a think about the task. When I come back you can tell me how you're going to go about doing it and what help you'll need from me."

Part two Ask your colleague to brief you on any modifications that should be made to the goal (where appropriate); the way they plan to approach the task; what help they will need from you; and when they would like to review progress. Once the task is complete, give your colleague feedback and pass a summary to the relevant manager where appropriate.

Maintaining momentum

Project work often requires effort over a prolonged period with little to show for it, so maintaining motivation can be a challenge. Procrastination is an ever-present danger, particularly on tasks that require high levels of concentration or challenging conversations with colleagues or clients.

Motivating yourself

Before you can start to motivate your team, you first have to motivate yourself; if you are not enthusiastic there is little chance that others will be. Do this by a combination of revisiting the end result—reminding yourself of its value and what it will be like to achieve it—and monitoring progress. Be sensitive to the first signs of procrastination and act quickly to ensure internal resistance is never given the chance to build up.

Decide what **one thing** you will do **immediately** to **progress the task,** and then do it

|01

|02

START SMALL

Begin by tackling as many **quick tasks** as possible, even if they are not the most important— this will give you a sense of **achievement** and keep you motivated.

REWARD YOURSELF

Write a to-do list and focus on one task at a time. When you have **completed** a task, **reward yourself.**

Beating mental blocks

Sometimes you can reach a point of near paralysis on a task. If this happens, try using this technique for reenergizing yourself: take a blank piece of paper and write the task on it. Then write for three minutes continuously about the task. Keep the pen moving, and jot down anything that comes to mind: why the task needs to be done; why you haven't done it; who else is involved; other ways of doing it; and steps for dealing with it. Now go through what you have written and highlight any insights or action points. Decide what one thing you will do immediately to progress the task—and then do it. Most people report an immediate rise in energy which, coupled with an increased understanding of the task, enables them to get over what had built into an insurmountable hurdle in their mind.

Tip

DON'T PROCRASTINATE
Avoid putting off challenging tasks—every time you do so, you put a brake on your **motivation** for the project as a whole.

LARGER PROJECTS
Break down projects that seem large and daunting into a series of small tasks. Set yourself **goals** and **time frames** for each task, and you will soon complete the project.

DIFFICULT TASKS
Challenging decisions and actions are often avoided, but **consider** what will happen if you do nothing. **Overcome your fear** and begin the task—it will help build your **confidence.**

Motivating others

Motivating your project team members can be difficult for a number of reasons:

- Long-term deadlines are always in danger of being pushed into the background by the distractions and crises of the day-to-day workload.
- Non-routine tasks are prone to procrastination.
- Team members may not see a connection between their effort on tasks, the project achieving its objective, and any benefit to them.
- People with a hierarchical mindset may resent doing work for a project manager who is less senior than them. Approach such people positively, but be prepared to escalate a problem as soon as you recognize that dealing with it will be beyond your capability.
- Team members working remotely can easily become isolated and feel disconnected from the project.

Take positive steps to motivate your team (see right), but also use your risk assessment to identify points where momentum may be lost, recording potential countermeasures in the risk log.

How to motivate your team

01
02
03
04

Selecting a medium for your message

HIGH

EMOTIONAL COMPLEXITY

LOW

Message: simple but emotionally charged, possibly requiring action from the recipient

Medium:
O Ad-hoc meeting
O Telephone conversation
O Private instant message chat
O Video call

Message: complex, with a high risk of misunderstanding or hurt feelings; need for the recipient to buy in to an idea and perhaps take action

Medium:
O Formal meeting
O Video conference

Message: simple, with a low risk of misunderstanding or hurt feelings; no need for high levels of emotional buy in

Medium:
O Instant message
O Email
O Note on the desk
O Voicemail message

Message: intellectually complex but emotionally noncontentious facts and figures

Medium:
O Email
O Letter

LOW   INTELLECTUAL COMPLEXITY   HIGH

Talking to your team

Maintain an open and honest relationship with your team. Keep in regular contact and listen carefully to concerns. Consider setting up a dedicated instant messaging channel for team members to stay in touch. In large teams, there is always a danger of people being left out of the loop when decisions are made. Ensure email distribution lists are up to date and make key documents available in one place, either on your network or on an online file-sharing platform such as Google Drive.

Choosing the method

Care is needed when selecting the medium by which you will communicate a particular message. Sending a sensitive message by email, for example, means that you run the risk of causing a potentially damaging misunderstanding with the recipient. Before pressing Send, take time to think about your purpose in communicating, what you want the outcome to be, and how complex the message is in emotional and intellectual terms.

Reviewing progress

Getting the team together is much easier and less costly in terms of time and resources now that everyone is used to video calls. Well-run review meetings are an essential ingredient in any project, offering you the opportunity to check past progress and confirm future direction. They also renew people's identification with your project team.

Keeping track of progress

An effective review meeting should be one part of a continuous cycle of activity. Prior to every meeting, all team members should work toward completing their tasks, and if they fail to do this within the set time frame, noncompletion should be reported to you. Use this information to formulate and circulate an agenda for the review meeting, with minutes of the last meeting attached as preparatory reading. At the meeting, start by discussing progress since your last review, then make decisions about what tasks need to be completed before the next time you meet. Delegate specific actions to members of the team. Record these actions in "Action minutes," which should be circulated as soon after the meeting as possible. This will give each individual the best chance of completing their tasks prior to the next meeting.

CHECKLIST...
Preparing to chair a review meeting **YES NO**

1 Are you **up to date** with all aspects of your own project work? (If your project work is behind schedule, you won't have the **authority** to chase others for theirs.) .... ☐ ☐

2 **Do you know** who will be there and how they are doing with the tasks they have been set? .... ☐ ☐

3 If the meeting is **taking place virtually,** have you made sure you can work the technology and that your backdrop is suitable? .... ☐ ☐

4 Are you **feeling calm?** (If you are stressed, this is likely to rub off on other people.) .... ☐ ☐

5 Are you **prepared to challenge** people who have not done what they are committed to, or who are behaving in a disruptive manner? .... ☐ ☐

RUNNING SUCCESSFUL REVIEWS

Dos	Dont's
O **Sending the agenda for the meeting in advance**	O Holding ad-hoc review meetings with no preparation
O **Ensuring that agenda items run to time, without having to be rushed**	O Allowing the discussion to wander and side issues to dominate
O **Allocating action points to attendees with agreed deadlines**	O Assuming that everyone will know what they have to do
O **Finishing with a discussion about what has been learned for next time**	O Accepting excuses without discussing how things can change

Scheduling review meetings

Review meetings can be scheduled as a regular event—at the same time of every day, for example, or on the same day of every week or month. Alternatively, the meetings can be fixed to the expected delivery date of certain products or to stages of the project. Both of these approaches have their strengths and weaknesses: regular meetings at the same time are more prone to "game playing" and a lack of concentration among attendees, but meetings set by the delivery dates of your project are more difficult to schedule to ensure that everyone can attend.

Tip

KEEP IT BRIEF

During busy periods, hold short "stand-up" **review meetings** early in the day, or at a point when most people would expect to be taking a break. Insist on a **prompt start, brief contributions,** and no deviation from the main purpose of reviewing progress and **coordinating activity** through the next period.

Managing project information

Whether project information exists on paper or as digital files—or a hybrid of the two—you'll want to have a good system in place so the team can readily find information and retrieve the latest version. Staying on top of this will save you time and stress in the long run.

Planning your system

Set up a system to manage your project documentation as part of the initiation phase of the project. Whether you use digital folders on a server or hard copies of paperwork, there are general steps to follow. When working online, create a clear file- and folder-naming protocol at the start and use it when adding any new documents to the system. If you're working on paper, compile a document schedule listing the records in your hard-copy folder in order, and place it at the front to save searching through. When you and your sponsor discuss the various records required at different points in the project, a shared screengrab of your online folder hierarchy or document schedule will help to structure the conversation.

Staying on track

01
02
03
04
05
06
07

Organizing the contents

Even small projects can generate large amounts of documentation, so plan how you organize folder contents carefully. Most project- and document-management software save past versions of documents and sync new versions in real time, allowing team members to collaborate on files. If your software doesn't, put your own version control in place. Give documents a version number manually and archive old versions away from information that is current and in regular use.

Organize documents that require a specific future action in date order, and use the reminder system in your electronic task list or calendar to flag important dates.

Tip

TAG YOUR DOCUMENTS

Whether you're working with digital or paper files, assign different **color tags** to different document types (records, contracts, reports, etc) so you and your team can **distinguish** between them at a glance.

FOLDER HIERARCHY

Place a document explaining your online folder hierarchy in a **prominent position** and instigate a **clear file-naming protocol** to help with retrieval and filing. If you're working with hard copies, keep a **document schedule** at the front of folders, like the index in a book.

TEAM ORGANIZATION DIAGRAM

Create a diagram—sometimes known as an organogram—setting out **who is doing what** in your team and the relationships between different people and jobs. Include **contact information**. This allows anyone to see whom they should approach on a particular matter.

DEFINITION DOCUMENTS

Keep a suite of documents that set out the **definition** of your project. This may include the **mandate, brief, business case**, PID, and any legal **contracts** or **client agreements**.

CHANGES TO SCOPE RECORDS

Keep digital or hard copies of these records close to the **definition documents** so that the material they contain is always accessed alongside the **original scope** to which they refer.

PROJECT PLAN AND BUDGET

Always ensure that you and your team are working from the most **up-to-date versions** of the **baseline plan** and **budget**. Archive intermediate versions elsewhere to avoid confusion.

RISK LOG

You will **refer** to this document almost as often as you do to your **plan and budget,** so make sure you keep the risk log up to date, with **constant review.**

SIGNIFICANT POINTS OF REFERENCE

After adding **live action points** to online task management to-do lists, it's still worth keeping **meeting minutes** that include significant points of reference in case questions arise over the decision-making timeline.

Monitoring costs

While it is important for you to monitor the schedule of the project and maintain focus on the outcome, it is equally vital that you keep track of the costs your project is incurring. Failure to do so can result in a project that, while seemingly successful is, in fact, uneconomic.

Managing project accounts

Effective cost monitoring throughout the lifecycle of a project is important for a number of reasons. It enables you to give the sponsor a true picture of progress whenever you are asked for it. It reduces risk by ensuring decisions to modify or cancel the project are taken early. It identifies areas of inefficiency, and it provides valuable information for planning future projects. Keeping track of your costs is also important because it could highlight theft or fraud. Like any other pot of money, project budgets occasionally attract criminal attention. If you are the person responsible for controlling expenditure, you may be liable unless you can demonstrate that you have used suitable procedures for monitoring costs.

How to monitor invisible costs

Use a **timesheet system** to keep track of time spent by your internal team.

Allocate a **financial value** to the time recorded on the timesheets.

Base calculations on the worker's salary broken down into an hourly rate.

Add in the **overhead cost** of employing that person (heating, lighting, office space, etc.)

Keeping track of costs

If you are managing a small project, you may not have a budget for out-of-pocket costs—paid to external organizations for materials or services—but you would do well to keep track of the invisible cost of the work undertaken by your internal team. Particularly in a multi-project environment, timesheets provide a mechanism for charging costs back to the right client or cost center. Out-of-pocket costs generally attract heavy scrutiny. Nevertheless this budget can come under pressure because of inaccurate estimates at the definition stage, additional features added to the scope without parallel increases in the budget, or poor risk management. If you are responsible for the budget, ensure you are clear on the reasons for any unforeseen expenditure before authorizing payment. Check the impact on other aspects of the budget: are you using money for desirable but nonessential features, leaving later essential features underfunded?

Tip

DON'T IGNORE HIDDEN COSTS

Beware of the seductive but potentially false **logic:** "We don't have the budget for that, we'll do it **ourselves.**"

Cost overruns

Not every cost overrun is serious—sometimes costs run ahead of plan simply because work is progressing more quickly than anticipated. On other occasions, you may have underestimated the cost of a "one-off" item of expenditure, but feel this is likely to be offset by an overestimate elsewhere. The point at which even a minor overspend should be taken seriously is when it is early warning that you have underestimated a whole class of activity upon which the project depends. Tell the sponsor as soon as you perceive that unforeseen costs may require an increase in the overall project budget. If the budget is fixed (critical), identify any nonessential features you can remove from the scope to bring costs back in line.

Case study

ADJUSTING TO CHANGE

The property department in a law firm won a contract to review 6,000 files for a local government agency. They priced the job at $1.5 million based on two hours per file after a start-up period. This proved accurate—experienced team members took just under two hours per file. However, the volume of work and tight schedule meant that morale dipped and staff turnover increased. The constant need to induct new staff pushed the average time per file for the first thousand files up to 2 hours 15 minutes. This would have caused the contract to overshoot by 12.5 percent, costing the firm $185k in lost revenue. The head of the department negotiated secondments from other departments to spread the workload, and offered incentives to raise morale. Thanks to the early intervention, productivity returned to less than two hours per file, and the project hit its projected profit margin.

Managing changes to scope

It is sometimes necessary to change or re-scope a project in order to adapt to circumstances that were not known when you drew up the definition. You must manage these changes carefully to avoid any misunderstanding among you, your sponsor, and the client.

Scope creep

The term "scope creep" is a term used to describe uncontrolled changes to the scope of a project. It is described as "creep" because the changes happen in such small steps that they go unnoticed until their true impact becomes apparent in the run-up to implementation. Sloppy project managers sometimes blame "scope creep" when they fail to deliver features that they should have spotted in the initial brief. However, it can also be caused by clients changing their minds or trying to get more than they have paid for in a commercial project.

Changes happen in such **small steps** that they go unnoticed until their **true impact** becomes apparent

Common reasons for changes to a project's scope

52%
of projects experience
scope creep

LOSS OF RESOURCES

The resources available to the project change (the budget is cut or increased, for example, or people with vital skills are moved out of or into the project team).

A RISK GOES BAD

The technology doesn't work, for example, or a legal hurdle cannot be overcome.

POOR PLANNING

It becomes apparent that the original scope is impossible to deliver within the set time or cost constraints.

NEW PERSONNEL

The client changes (a new person comes in with new ideas).

INDECISION

The client changes their mind about what they want.

ADDED BENEFITS

New facts or technological advances would enable the project to deliver valuable additional benefits if the scope were modified.

USAGE CHANGE

The circumstances in which the end product will be used have changed.

96%

of organizations believe they will need to be **more agile** in the future **to be successful**

Defining the change

The golden rule when re-scoping a project is to confirm all changes of scope in writing with the project sponsor. By creating a written record of all changes you create an audit trail that ensures that you and the sponsor have the same understanding of what the change is and why you are making it. Never agree to a change in scope before carrying out a full impact assessment, to identify how other features of the product will be affected, and developing a costed plan for how to deliver the change.

US$99

million **is lost for every US$1 billion** invested due to **poor project performance**

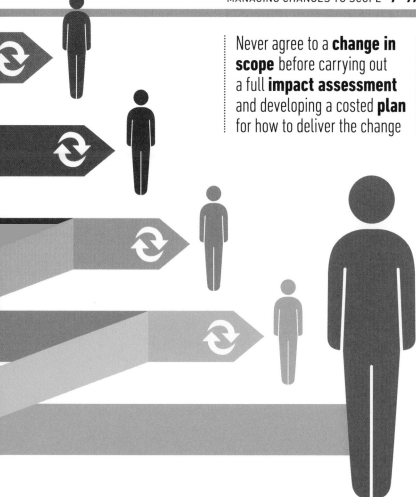

Never agree to a **change in scope** before carrying out a full **impact assessment** and developing a costed **plan** for how to deliver the change

Communicating change

Communicate changes to all those involved in the project's delivery as well as those who will receive the end product. If your organization does not have a standard "Changes to Scope" document format and you decide to create one, ensure it has a similar format to the original scoping document so that

they can be compared easily and any specific modifications highlighted. The document should be signed off by the client—to ensure that he or she wants the change; by you, to confirm that you can deliver it; and by the sponsor who ultimately has the authority to sanction the change.

Going
live

At the end of every project, there comes a point at which whatever it has produced needs to be handed over to the end users. As the culmination of all your efforts, this should be an exciting time for the project manager, but there will also be challenges to face, and careful management is required to deliver a smooth handover and a successful outcome.

04

Implementing the project

Ensuring that the client, the team, and your organization have a positive experience as your project "goes live" is one of a project manager's most important responsibilities. The decisions you make during every phase of your project's life cycle should be with implementation in mind.

Overcoming challenges

Implementation is primarily a client-focused phase of a project. However, you should also consider its significance for the end user, the project team, and your organization. As the project goes live, end users have to assimilate changes and come out of their comfort zone, while project team members have to let go of a project and move on to something new. Your organization simply wants swift and trouble-free implementation in order to realize the benefits of their investment. Your role as project manager is to help all three groups deal with these challenges.

89%

of projects in US
high-performing
organizations are
completed

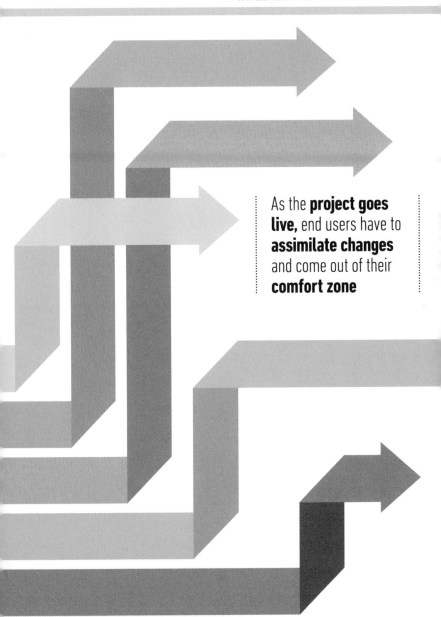

As the **project goes live,** end users have to **assimilate changes** and come out of their **comfort zone**

Key actions for successful implementation

PHASE OF PROJECT

INITIATION PHASE

Describe the issue to be addressed or opportunity to be exploited.

DEFINITION PHASE

Design an end product that satisfies the need identified in initiation.

PLANNING PHASE

Design a communications plan that delivers the information that different stakeholders need, and ensure the resources are available for successful implementation.

CONTROL PHASE

Ensure all stakeholders are kept informed on progress and manage people's expectations.

IMPLEMENTATION PHASE

Present the product in the most positive way possible, demonstrating an understanding of all stakeholders' needs.

Plan in time and budget for **implementation activities** such as **rehearsals, marketing, training, and change management**

ACTIONS

- **Conduct research** among end users to establish how widespread the issue or opportunity is.
- **Document findings** and, where confidentiality allows, **circulate** them to those who contributed.

- Wherever possible, **design the product** in consultation with the client/end user—attribute good ideas to those who offered them.
- Give an **indicative date** for implementation.
- Use prototypes and mock-ups to **bring the idea alive** both for the client and the project team.

- Find out what **aspects of progress** the stakeholders are interested in and how frequently they want reports, then create a **communications plan** to deliver this.
- Plan in time and budget for **implementation activities** such as rehearsals, marketing, training, and change management.
- **Book facilities,** equipment, and personnel required for implementation as soon as you have a launch timetable.

- **Deliver the communications plan,** and take advantage of any unexpected opportunities to promote your project.
- **Find opportunities** for listening to stakeholders' **hopes** and concerns.
- Tell all stakeholders about any **changes to the product** or launch date, explaining why these have occurred.
- **Create the materials** (documentation, guides, manuals, etc.) required to support implementation.
- Train those who will **support the product** once it has gone live.
- Recruit end users who will **test the product** as soon as it is ready for implementation.
- **Plan and rehearse** implementation events.

- Get end users to **test** what you have produced **(User Acceptance Testing).**
- Hold **implementation events** to roll out the end product.
- **Train or brief end users** and distribute supporting documentation as necessary.
- Get the sponsor to **inspect** the finished product and **sign it off** as complete.
- Hold a **celebratory event** with the project team.
- Reassign project personnel, **providing feedback** to them and their managers as appropriate.

Preparing for handover

Although the majority of work has been done, projects can sometimes stall at the implementation stage. You may run out of budget, or lose members of your team to other projects, or there may be last-minute changes from the client as they realize that implementation is imminent. Careful management at this stage ensures that your handover to the end users goes as smoothly as possible.

Managing the final stages

As a project nears completion, team members can often feel jaded; the novelty that drew them to the project in the first place has become a distant memory. To reinvigorate your team, hold a pre-implementation meeting with all those involved, including clients and end users wherever possible. The core purpose of this meeting is to produce a detailed route map through to completion, but a well-run meeting can do wonders for your team's motivation and focus—especially if they see the client's enthusiasm for what you are about to deliver.

Steering the end game

Your role leading up to implementation is primarily one of problem-solving and coordination of the activity required for the project to "go live." Check in with all stakeholders, particularly team members. Show an interest in what

> **Tip**
>
> **HOLD ON TO YOUR TEAM**
> Tell **team members** that they are finished on your project only when you are absolutely **clear** that this is the case.

they are doing but resist the temptation to step in unless they really cannot do what has been asked of them without your help. Increase the frequency of review as you get close to your final date, but do not allow these meetings to get in the way of the work they should be doing. A 10-minute "stand-up" meeting may work best, either in person, or using a video-conferencing app if you have team members working remotely. Conference calls also work well.

10 **minutes** may be sufficient **time** for **review meetings** in the **final** project stages

Running final tests

For some projects, User Acceptance Testing (UAT) is one of the last steps before implementation. Most frequently found in software development—as the final technical test of a product—UAT may also be applied in a variety of situations. The testing is carried out by a representative panel of end users, who work through as many different scenarios as necessary to be sure that the product will perform as expected when it goes live. UAT must not be used to confirm that the product is what the end users want—that should have been defined in the project scope and any subsequent "changes to scope" documents.

Hold a **pre-implementation meeting** with all those involved, including **clients** and **end users**

How to hold a pre-implementation meeting

Review the original scope of your project, and talk through the plan you have used to achieve it.

Make a detailed implementation plan, using the team planning technique that you used to generate the overall plan.

Create a project closure checklist, with detailed timings and responsibilities, in a form that can be used to chart progress.

This serves as a reminder of why the **project is important** and highlights how much has been achieved.

Encourage creativity, and make it your business to secure the resources needed to **deliver a successful** handover.

Make sure everyone leaves the meeting knowing precisely what they have to do and by when.

Handing over the project

The way in which a project "goes live" varies according to the nature of its product. With time-critical projects, there is rarely any doubt about the "go live" point, but where quality is the critical factor, the opposite is often the case, and it takes a conscious effort to mark the point at which a project is complete.

Signaling the end point

Projects are different to business as usual because they have an end point at which they can be declared complete and then have their success evaluated. Even if you are the only person working on a project, it is still helpful to mark the "go live" point. This will send a clear signal that the project is finished and that you and the rest of the project team will be moving on.

For most projects, implementation should coincide with the transference of responsibility from the project team to an ongoing support function. The better you and your team have managed the client while the project was underway, the more difficult you will find it to get them to transfer their allegiance to a new group. By marking the "go live" point, you make a definitive statement to your client that the time has come for this to happen.

> By marking the **"go live"** point, you make a definitive statement to your **client**

CHECKLIST...
Marking "go live"   YES NO

1 Have I made a **clear declaration** to all stakeholders
that the project is complete? .... ☐ ☐

2 Have I **clearly signaled** to the client and end users that
they are now responsible for the product? .... ☐ ☐

3 Have I **marked the point** at which project personnel are
available for other assignments? .... ☐ ☐

4 Have I taken the **opportunity to say thank you** to those who
have contributed to the project? .... ☐ ☐

Case study

GREASING THE WHEELS

A project manager charged with moving 40 people from an office in the heart of the West End of London to more spacious but cheaper premises in a less affluent part of the city faced a challenge to ensure smooth implementation: the move was for financial reasons and no one wanted to go. He decided to put together a welcome pack for each member of staff, and asked every shop, bar, café, restaurant, and gym in the area around the new offices whether they would make introductory offers to the newcomers when they showed their company ID cards. On the day of the move, he placed the finished pack of discounted goods and services on each desk in the new offices. The offers it contained actively encouraged people to explore the area rather than simply sitting at their desks and complaining about their new surroundings. And when they did take up the offers, they found that they were welcomed as a valuable customer.

Holding an event

Hold a "go live" event (perhaps couched as a final review meeting) to review the whole project. Evaluate the changes and benefits it has achieved. Consider how to organize the event so that there are things to see, do, and talk about. Make sure it is appropriate, though: if you overplay going live, you may be accused of showing off. Involve the project sponsor in the event and thank all those who have contributed.

Another pretext for an event might be to introduce the client or end users to the people who are about to begin supporting them. Reiterate the post-implementation support that will be available and how snagging will take place. Snagging is the process of identifying and resolving minor defects that takes place during the implementation phase, prior to the project being declared complete. Make sure that everyone understands the part you need them to play in bedding the project in.

Providing support

In a quality-critical project, the quality of post-implementation support given to the end user is essential to its long-term success. Never declare a project complete until the end user has been trained to use the product and first-line support is available from outside the project team.

Tip

TAKE ADVICE

Speak to your **sponsor** about your plans for marking **"go live."** Ultimately it is up to him or her to decide when the project is complete.

Evaluating success

Once the end product has been delivered, the project manager's final act should be to review the outcome of the project and evaluate its overall success. It can often be illuminating to make this post-implementation review against both the original scope and any subsequent modifications.

Analyzing the outcome

You should review the success of your project in a number of ways. First, look at your immediate impression: did the project deliver what was expected? This level of review is best done at the same time as implementation—in fact, it should be part of the sign-off procedure involving sponsor, client, and project manager. The review process should also look at whether the project has delivered a long-term benefit. In time-critical projects, this may already be at least partly evident at implementation or shortly afterward, but in quality-critical projects the benefits may take longer to become clear. Finally, your evaluation should look at the benefits gained in business terms. Was the project worth it financially?

GIVE A PERSONAL REWARD

Send an appropriate gift to members of the team at their homes with a personalized note: a bunch of **flowers,** gift certificates for a spa, or **tickets for an event** can all deliver **a much bigger message** than the money that they cost.

GIVE BONUSES

Team members will always appreciate **a cash bonus,** if funds are available.

Tip

INVOLVE THE SPONSOR
Try to get the sponsor involved in the **review process**—experience suggests that without their **involvement,** the review rarely gets done, as people are busy and move on to the next job.

Did the **project** deliver what was **expected?** Was the project worth it **financially?**

GIVE A PROJECT GIFT

Give **a tailor-made** project present to thank people for taking part. This **gift** does not have to be expensive but should be tasteful, fun, and/or useful.

EXPRESS YOUR THANKS

Hand-write a personal letter to each team member expressing **thanks** for his or her personal **contribution,** making the effort to **write something different** in each one.

COMMEMORATE THE OCCASION

Write an article for your in-house e-newsletter or your organization's website. Remember to **thank all the team** and show how their work helped to **achieve aims** and **benefit** the whole organization.

Ideas for celebrating success

ALLOCATE FUNDS

Put a small **"celebration fund"** into the project budget, which increases or decreases depending on whether the project is in front or behind time and budget. At the end of the project, hold **a social event,** involving everyone who contributed, at which you and the sponsor (and client if appropriate) can express your thanks.

67%

of well-formulated **strategies fail** because of **poor execution**

Reviewing the process

A "lessons learned" review allows you to learn from the process you have been through and helps you find ways to improve your project management. Because the project process should be repeatable, the main purpose of review is to establish what went well, what could have gone better, and what you can do to improve future projects.

Looking back at your project

The review process is your chance to learn from experience. It is not just about spotting errors or identifying parts of the process that did not run as smoothly as they could have—evaluation of what was successful is equally informative. If something worked particularly well (such as a technique or a supplier), it should be noted for future reference.

However, inevitably there will be some things that go wrong in your projects, and these also provide valuable lessons for the future. Although they may have been unforeseeable the first time they occurred, by taking the time to understand what has happened and why, you should be able to gain insights that would otherwise be missed, and take action to prevent their recurrence in future projects.

> If something **worked** particularly well (such as a technique or a supplier), it should **be noted** for **future reference**

69%
of projects meet their original **goals and business intent**

Learning from the details

When reviewing the project, consider all aspects of the process in detail. Do not rely on opinions about what went well or make assumptions about what went wrong: talk to those involved and try to discover the facts. When these are in dispute, ask for evidence. Be curious about why things happened, and explore how this could inform future project decisions. When searching for the

PLANNING PROJECTS FOR LEARNING

Dos	Don'ts
O **Establishing quality assurance procedures from the outset**	O Allowing an experienced project team to perform their roles out of habit
O **Giving personal learning objectives for the project to all team members**	O Being cynical about the organization's ability to do things differently
O **Including "lessons learned" as a regular agenda item for meetings**	O Considering change a threat to what has been successful in the past
O **Having a team culture characterized by high levels of feedback**	O Allowing a blame culture, in which it is dangerous to admit mistakes
O **Establishing mechanisms for disseminating new ideas**	O Holding the project plan centrally and discouraging discussion of its details

truth, be sensitive to the feelings of those involved: reviews should never become witch hunts.

Once you have a good understanding of how everything worked, make sure that you act on your findings. Project learning is done for a purpose—to improve performance on future projects. Don't keep useful information and ideas to yourself—pass them on to where they can make a difference.

Holding a project review

A "lessons learned" review meeting is your opportunity to get the team together and discuss how the project went. Hold the meeting as soon as implementation is complete—you can always call a second one, if necessary, once the project has bedded in. Far from duplicating effort, you will find that you actually save time using this approach, because memories are clearer and conclusions are reached more quickly.

Involve as many stakeholders as is practical in this meeting. A process review should take account of the views of everyone involved, but within the constraints of cost, time, and availability. If possible, include the views of the client and end user, although in commercial projects, you may need to think carefully about how you are going to get these.

Be clear on what you want to achieve and have an agenda for the meeting. A review meeting can become unfocused and descend into generalizations unless there are specific items to discuss. If you have held interim learning reviews, use the notes from these as a structure. If not, then the PID, plan, and risk log can be a good basis for discussion.

> Aim for three **key learning points** clearly described so that anyone encountering a similar problem in the future can **implement your recommendations**

Tip

PLAN AHEAD
Set a date for the review meeting when you are **planning** the implementation of the project— this should make it easier to get the time in people's calendars.

Documenting your review

Brevity is often the key to a successful project review document, so record the recommendations that you generate following the "lessons learned" review meeting succinctly. Aim for three key learning points clearly described so that anyone encountering a similar problem in the future can implement your recommendations. If you have to write more because the project was large and complex, structure the document in a way that enables people to gain an overview quickly and then select only the detail that is relevant to them. It can be useful to generate a main document that you distribute to all stakeholders— containing a limited number of key recommendations for the conduct of future projects—and a number of annexes. These can either cover each recommendation in detail or provide more detailed feedback to specific individuals or departments.

Discuss your recommendations with the sponsor. Even if the sponsor does not want to be fully involved in the review process, at the very least you should discuss the findings with him or her before disseminating them to a wider audience.

ASK YOURSELF...
What can we learn from this project?   **YES** **NO**

1 Was our **original scope good?** .... ☐ ☐

2 Were the time and cost estimates **accurate?** .... ☐ ☐

3 Did we have the **right mix** of people on our team? .... ☐ ☐

4 Did the stakeholders **work together effectively?** .... ☐ ☐

5 Might we have **anticipated risks** better? .... ☐ ☐

6 Did the **technology** we used **perform effectively?** .... ☐ ☐

7 Did our **project methodology** work well? .... ☐ ☐

8 Were our project documents **useful?** Were any missing? .... ☐ ☐

Giving personal feedback

The review phase of your project should also look at the performance of individual members of your team. Although you should have been giving regular feedback throughout the project, people appreciate a final review once it is completed, especially when they've put a lot of effort into making a project successful. You will find that the best workers use feedback from project reviews as a way to build their CV or gather testimonials. Equally, people will be more likely to make a second effort if they know that failure will be investigated and recorded.

Tip

THINK SMALL
Don't underestimate **the value** of small, easily implemented improvements to your approach. A **"lessons learned"** review should identify several of these, and their combined effect can be **significant.**

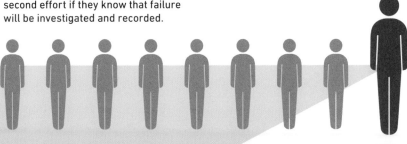

Index

Acknowledgments

Stats

p.10 PWC Insights and Trends: Current Portfolio, Programme, and Project Management Practices survey 2012

p.16 PMI's Pulse of the Profession 2014: The High Cost of Low Performance

p.29 PMI's Pulse of the Profession 2017: Success Rates Rise: Transforming the High Cost of Low Performance

p.35 e-meetings.verizonbusiness.com/global/en/meetingsinamerica/uswhitepaper.php

p.36 KPMG, AIPM and IPMA's The Future of Project Management: Global Outlook 2019

p.40 Wellingtone The State of Project Management survey 2021

p.42 Wellingtone The State of Project Management survey 2021

p.46 PWC Insights and Trends: Current Portfolio, Programme, and Project Management Practices survey 2012

p.49 Wellingtone The State of Project Management survey 2021

p.59 Gallup Employee Burnout: Causes and Cures report

p.65 Live Career: Is Remote Work Here to Stay? study 2021

p.65 blog.bonus.ly/the-state-of-employee-engagement-2019

p.75 PMI's Pulse of the Profession 2018: Success in Disruptive Times: Expanding the Value Delivery Landscape to Address the High Cost of Low Performance

p.76 IESE Business School & Oliver Wyman "Organizational Agility" study 2018

p.76 PMI's Pulse of the Profession 2018: Success in Disruptive Times: Expanding the Value Delivery Landscape to Address the High Cost of Low Performance

p.80 PMI's Pulse of the Profession 2014: The High Cost of Low Performance

p.89 Bridges Strategy Implementation 2016 Survey Results

p.90 PMI's Pulse of the Profession 2017: Success Rates Rise: Transforming the High Cost of Low Performance

Second edition:

Senior Art Editor Gillian Andrews
Project Editor Hugo Wilkinson
Designer XAB Design
Editor Louise Tucker
UK Editor Sam Kennedy
US Editors Margaret Parrish, Jill Hamilton
Managing Editor Stephanie Farrow
Senior Managing Art Editor Lee Griffiths
Production Editor Nikoleta Parasaki
Production Controller Mandy Inness
Jacket Designer Mark Cavanagh
Design Development Manager Sophia M.T.T.

Delhi Team:

Senior Art Editor Govind Mittal
Art Editor Vikas Chauhan
DTP Designer Vishal Bhatia

First edition:

Senior Editor Peter Jones
Senior Art Editor Helen Spencer
Executive Managing Editor Adèle Hayward
Managing Art Editor Kat Mead
Art Director Peter Luff
Publisher Stephanie Jackson
Production Editor Ben Marcus
Production Controller Hema Gohil
US Editor Margaret Parrish

First edition produced for
Dorling Kindersley Limited by
Cobalt ID
The Stables, Wood Farm,
Deopham Road,
Attleborough, Norfolk NR17 1AJ
www.cobaltid.co.uk

Editors

Louise Abbott, Kati Dye,
Maddy King, Marek Walisiewicz